Toys Can Teach

by Carmel Reilly

Toys Can Teach

Toys are fun. They can teach us, too.

Children love playing with toys.

There are lots of different toys.
Some toys teach skills.

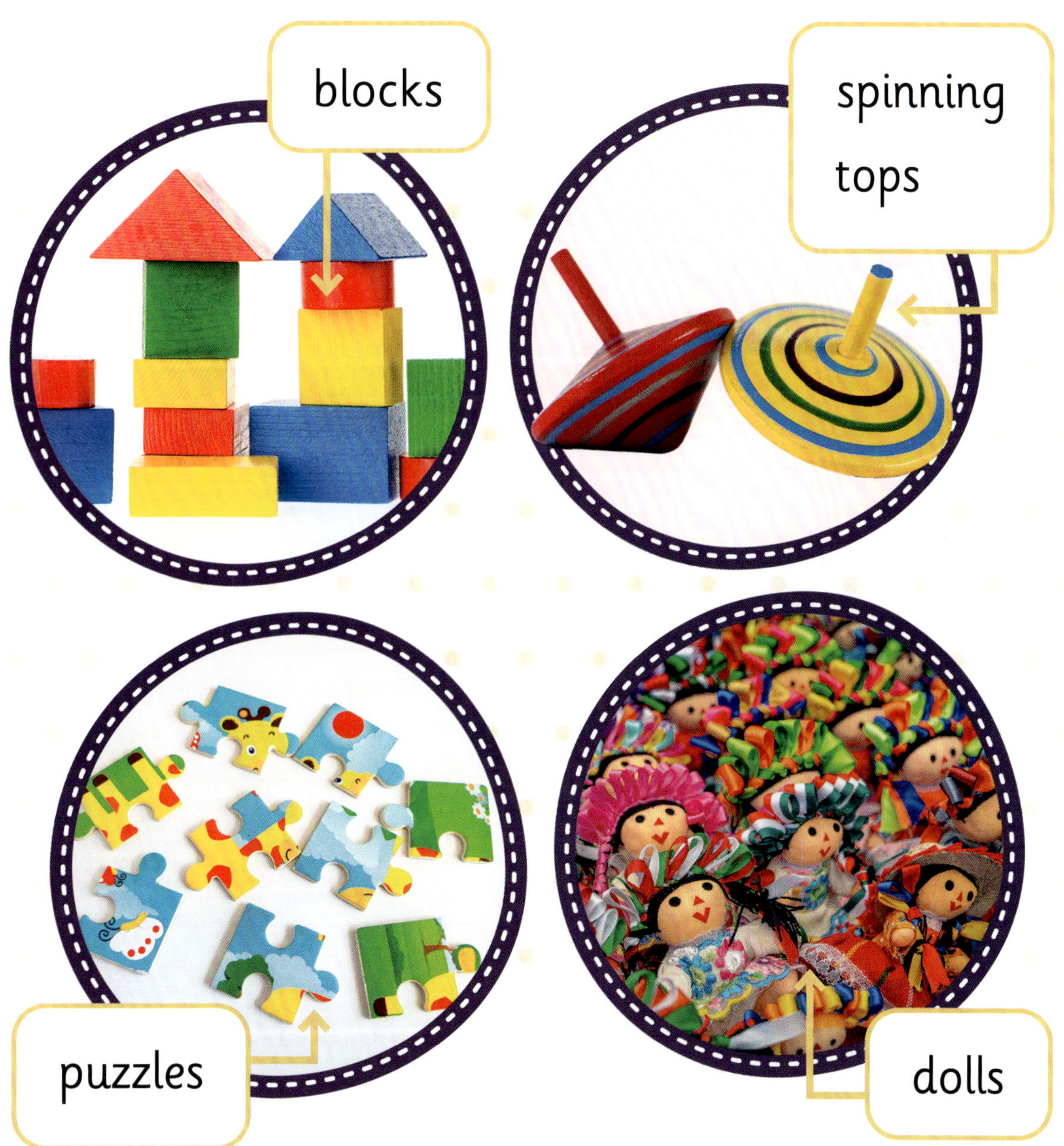

Blocks

Blocks can be big or little. Blocks can be wooden or plastic.

Children enjoy blocks.

Children can do lots with blocks.

Blocks teach us to **stack**.

This girl stacks blocks high.

Blocks show how to sort. **Sorting** is an important skill.

The boy puts blocks in order.

Playing with blocks teaches counting.

She counts out the blocks.

Some blocks are little bricks. They can be joined.

Look at this brick statue.

Puzzles

Some puzzles teach sorting.

You sort beads in this puzzle.

Doing puzzles teaches children to think.

Puzzles can be difficult.

Some things are hidden in puzzles.
You must look for them.

Can you see the fawn?

You can look for clues in puzzles.
You need to think hard.

Can this bit fit?

Spinning Tops

It is fun to spin tops.

There are big and little spinning tops.

Children enjoy seeing tops spin. Tops seem to twirl forever.

Twirling tops teaches children. It helps with their **hand skills**.

Spinning a top is a skill.

Tops can be hard to spin. You need the right spot.

Firm ground is good.

Dolls

Playing with dolls can teach children.

There are all sorts of dolls.

Children dress their dolls.

The doll is dressed in a skirt.

It is cold. The girl has put a shawl on her doll.

Children put on plays for people. Puppets act out the play.

This venue has a puppet show.

The boy **tends to** his doll.

He fixes his doll with glue.

Skills from Playing with Toys

Skills	
stacking	✔
sorting	✔
counting	✔
thinking	✔
hand	✔

Toys are a lot of fun. Toys teach so much too.

What do toys teach you?

Look It Up

hand skills: doing something well with your hands

sorting: putting things in order

stack: put on top of

tends to: looks after

Index